CYBERATTACKS and CYBERSCAMS

Is There an End in Sight?

Jennifer Stephan

ReferencePoint
Press®

San Diego, CA

About the Author

Jennifer Stephan writes nonfiction books and articles for tweens and teens. Her work explores how people change and are changed by the communities and times in which they live. She earned a PhD in human development and social policy from Northwestern University and has worked as an education policy researcher. She lives outside Chicago with her husband and daughters.

For more information, contact:
ReferencePoint Press, Inc.
PO Box 27779
San Diego, CA 92198
www.ReferencePointPress.com

Picture Credits:
Cover: freedomzaik/Shutterstock

6: Associated Press
11: fizkes/Shutterstock.com
12: SpeedKingz/Shutterstock
14: tkyszk/Shutterstock
18: Sharkshock/Shutterstock
22: Rawpixel.com/Shutterstock
25: Associated Press

28: Valeriya Zankovych/Shutterstock
30: Associated Press
33: pongky.n/iStock
38: GaudiLab/iStock
41: Alex Edelman/Sipa/Newscom
43: BrandonKleinPhoto/Shutterstock.com
48: Mikhail Metzel/Zuma Press/Newscom
50: Andrey Arkusha/Shutterstock
54: Hugo Amaral/Zuma Press/Newscom

LIBRARY OF CONGRESS CATALOGING-IN-PUBLICATION DATA

Names: Stephan, Jennifer, author.
Title: Cyberattacks and cyberscams : is there an end in sight? / by Jennifer Stephan.
Description: San Diego, CA : ReferencePoint Press, Inc., 2023. | Includes bibliographical references and index.
Identifiers: LCCN 2021051538 (print) | LCCN 2021051539 (ebook) | ISBN 9781678203283 (library binding) | ISBN 9781678203290 (ebook)
Subjects: LCSH: Computer fraud--United States--Juvenile literature. | Internet fraud--United States--Juvenile literature. | Swindlers and swindling--United States--Juvenile literature.
Classification: LCC HV6773.15.C56 S74 2023 (print) | LCC HV6773.15.C56 (ebook) | DDC 364.16/3--dc23/eng/20211021
LC record available at https://lccn.loc.gov/2021051538
LC ebook record available at https://lccn.loc.gov/2021051539

Contents

Cyberscams and Cyberattacks Surge

As Americans rummaged through closets for red, white, and blue to wear and wave for their 2021 Independence Day celebrations, a notorious Russia-based cybergang launched its own fireworks. Just before the July 4 holiday weekend, REvil (short for Ransomware Evil) hackers embedded ransomware into an update from Kaseya, a US-based software provider with tens of thousands of clients worldwide. The ransomware infected Kaseya's business customers and then spilled down the supply chain to infect the customers of Kaseya's customers. The single blow impacted hundreds of organizations. The ransomware encrypted files and demanded a ransom from each customer for the release of their files. Town officials, librarians, dentists, and other victims lost access to records, billing systems, emails, and anything else stored on their computers. The ransomware shot around the globe, hitting a hospital in Romania, freezing computers at schools in New Zealand, and bringing down about seven hundred Swedish grocery stores. Soon after the attack, according to the cybersecurity company Sophos, REvil gloated on its website that it had infected over 1 million devices. For $70 million in Bitcoin, REvil promised to provide Kaseya a universal decryptor, which Kaseya could then provide to its customers.

The REvil ransomware had been used before, but the Kaseya attack unsettled even seasoned observers. "The scale and scope of this attack is really unprecedented,"[1] says cybersecurity expert Dmitri Alperovitch. The criminals showed a technical sophistication only nation-states usually achieve. Some victims dusted off backups they may never have imagined needing. Others wondered if they would recover at all.

> "The more digital connections people make and data they exchange, the more opportunities adversaries have to destroy private lives, disrupt critical infrastructure, and damage our economic and democratic institutions."[2]
>
> —Cyberspace Solarium Commission

Twenty days after detecting the attack, Kaseya announced that, although it had not paid the ransom, it had obtained a universal decryptor. It was later revealed that the Federal Bureau of Investigation (FBI) had provided the decryptor, which it obtained by accessing REvil's servers. In late October 2021, law enforcement officials and cybersecurity professionals from the United States and other countries turned the tables. They hacked REvil, shutting down its operations, at least temporarily.

Cyberspace brings trade-offs. Connectivity has boosted economic productivity, improved education, enhanced social interactions, and created new forms of entertainment. But it also makes people and things vulnerable. As the Cyberspace Solarium Commission, established by Congress to develop a national cybersecurity strategy, explains, "The more digital connections people make and data they exchange, the more opportunities adversaries have to destroy private lives, disrupt critical infrastructure, and damage our economic and democratic institutions."[2] There is no end in sight to cyberscams or cyberattacks. But experts believe Americans can reduce the number of scams and attacks and also build resilience to recover from them more quickly.

Cyberoffense

Cyberscams and cyberattacks seem increasingly common. In 2020 the FBI received almost eight hundred thousand complaints

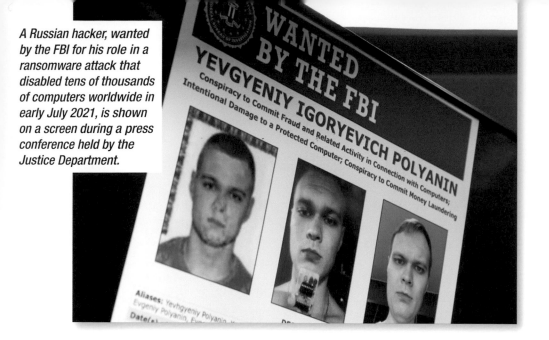

of cyberscams, a 69 percent increase from 2019. Ransomware attacks have also ballooned. Victims paid nearly $350 million in 2020, over three times as much as in 2019, according to crypto-currency analytics firm Chainalysis. Criminals carry out scams and ransomware attacks for profit. Nation-states launch cyberattacks both for espionage and for sabotage. According to the Council on Foreign Relations, there were seventy-six state-sponsored cyber-attacks in 2019, mostly espionage related.

Cyberaggressions by scammers, criminals, and nation-states have direct and spillover effects. Although many scams result in small financial losses, some devastate individuals financially and emotionally. Ransomware and nation-state attacks have crip-pled businesses, institutions, and governments. They have also harmed economies and could threaten national security. As the technological sophistication of nation-states grows, so do the risks of bad outcomes. Speaking to the Office of the Director of National Intelligence, President Joe Biden said, "I think it's more likely . . . if we end up in a war, a real shooting war with a major power, it's going to be as a consequence of a cyber breach of great consequence."[3] Cybertechnology has supercharged tradi-tional crimes and international aggressions. It has also enabled new kinds of scams, extortion, and nation-state attacks.

Cyberdefense

Cyberscams and ransomware attacks offer criminals easy and reliable profits. Cybertechnology also gives nation-states a relatively low-cost way to spy on or harm adversaries. To deter scams and attacks, defenders try to raise the costs and lower the expected payoffs of cyberaggressions. Better collaboration between the private and public sectors could help with that. Increased cooperation among nation-states can make the payoffs of cyberaggression less dependable.

Even the best defense will not eradicate cyberassaults. Individuals, organizations, and governments need to build resilience. Procedures that mitigate damage, as well as response plans that allow for quicker recovery, can help. If significant steps to improve cybersecurity are not taken, experts warn, future July 4 explosions may not be fireworks.

Every time another person connects a thermostat, doorbell, or baby monitor to the internet, the attack surface grows. A future of autonomous vehicles and smart cities could drastically increase vulnerabilities. Cybersecurity experts Richard A. Clarke and Robert K. Knake, whose combined experience includes advising three American presidents, believe cyberattacks will never end completely. "The goal is to achieve a state of ongoing improvement, where systems are continually being made more secure and the work of attacking these systems is harder, takes longer, and comes with greater risk of failure and punishment."[4] Although cyberscams and cyberattacks may be inevitable, making scams and attacks more costly to launch and the proceeds less certain will help reduce their number. Building resilience will make them hurt less.

> "I think it's more likely . . . if we end up in a war, a real shooting war with a major power, it's going to be as a consequence of a cyber breach of great consequence."[3]
>
> —President Joe Biden

Chapter One

Cyberscams

Like your favorite brand of ice cream, cyberscams come in dozens of flavors. They range from "spray and pray" email blasts that try to reach many people with a basic message to elaborately customized ruses with characters and backstory. "Anyone can become a victim of a cyber fraud or scam, if targeted in the right way at the right time by a highly skilled offender,"[5] say researchers Mark Button and Cassandra Cross. Cybertechnology makes traditional scams more effective and efficient. It also enables new kinds of fraud. Scams differ in their content and targets, but they use similar strategies to accomplish the same goal: obtain something of value from the target. It could be cash, assistance in laundering money, or something to trade for cash—such as personal data, passwords, or contacts. Among the most prominent scams are employment, confidence, online shopping, and identity fraud.

Employment Fraud

When teen Elisa Chavez wanted to earn money for college, she searched the online job listings. She investigated every lead but without success, Chavez told CBS Chicago. After a month, an opportunity finally arrived by text. It asked if she was interested in interviewing for a remote administrative position. Chavez checked the names of the recruiters. She saw that they matched the names of employees at Medline, a local company. She agreed to the interview, which lasted about an hour on

Fleep, a messaging app. The recruiters promised to reach out, and soon she heard good news. Chavez got the job. She received a formal letter with Medline's logo splashed across the top and paperwork to complete. Chavez provided copies of her ID card, bank account number, and Social Security number, all information employers typically request from a new employee.

But then—silence. "[I] just felt queasy like something was not right,"[6] Chavez says. She texted the recruiters, but they did not respond. She checked the Fleep account, but it had been deleted. When she went to Medline's online career center, she noticed something she had missed earlier. The email addresses of Medline employees ended in "@medline.com," not "@medlinejobs.com" like the addresses of her so-called recruiters. Realization struck. She had fallen for a scam, and now the fake employers had some of her most valuable personal data.

The Better Business Bureau (BBB) ranks employment fraud among the top three riskiest cyberscams. Employment scammers convince victims that they are applying to, being hired by, or working for a legitimate employer. The scams often involve detailed setups such as job postings on legitimate recruiting websites, interviews and forms, and props like logos, websites, or email addresses that appear authentic. An elaborate setup helped convince Chavez to hand over her personal data, something she might never have done in other circumstances. With a victim's personal and financial information, criminals can make purchases or apply for credit cards, loans, tax refunds, and employment benefits.

In another type of employment fraud, scammers offer targets a job on the condition that they buy their own supplies or pay for training. After victims pay, the fake employer and job disappear. Still other employment scams trick victims into money laundering;

for example, by hiring someone to receive and ship stolen goods. Even young and technologically adept people like Chavez can fall for cyberscams.

Confidence Fraud

Confidence fraud is another prominent type of scam with different variations. Reporter Hugh Lessig found out just how heartbreaking romance scams can be when he interviewed a woman he calls "Jennifer." Jennifer met a soldier on Facebook just before he deployed to Afghanistan. They kept in touch. Over months, they built a relationship from shared stories and confidences, but only hers were real. Teetering on a rocky point in her marriage, it was easy to fall for the impostor. "[He] told me . . . how much he would like to meet me, how pretty I was, how nice I was," she told Lessig. "He would tell me stories about the war and things that were going on. I felt so bad for him . . . I wanted to do whatever I could to make life easier for him."[7] When the fake soldier asked for money, Jennifer sent some. Then she sent more and more, until she had given the scammer $4,000. The soldier was not real. The romance was not real, but the loss was real.

Romance scams rank among the costliest frauds. The median loss was $2,100 in 2020, according to the BBB. Romance scammers fabricate a relationship with a victim and then trick the victim into sending money, laundering money, or disclosing personal data. Some romance scammers prey on the elderly and can drain their entire life savings. But it is not just the loss of money that hurts the most. "With this fraud, especially, there is so much emotional trauma," says Amy Nofziger from the AARP Fraud Watch Network. "They're embarrassed. Their hearts are broken. They not only lost their money, but this dream they had."[8]

"With this fraud, especially, there is so much emotional trauma. . . . They're embarrassed. Their hearts are broken. They not only lost their money, but this dream they had."[8]

—Amy Nofziger, director of Victim Support at the AARP Fraud Watch Network

Romance scams begin with a fake profile on a dating app or social media account. Many scammers impersonate soldiers. Soldiers seem trustworthy. They can also be stationed far away, have little control over their schedules, and need to keep secrets—all good excuses to avoid meeting in person or answering too many questions. Next, scammers find targets. They may cast a wide net at first, then pursue the most promising victims. Scammers can pluck clues out of online profiles to tailor their approach. Through messages, photos, and calls, scammers build fake relationships with their victims. Eventually, scammers ask for money, perhaps starting with a small request such as a gift card to purchase cell phone minutes. Soon the requests swell—funds for an emergency or tickets to meet in person. If a victim tries to break things off, some scammers turn verbally abusive. In another version of romance fraud, a scammer convinces the victim to provide compromising videos and then uses them for extortion.

Confidence scams do not always entail romance. Scammers may instead impersonate a target's friend or relative on the phone or in an email and ask for emergency money. To make the scenario more realistic, scammers sometimes lace their stories

11

with details taken from targets' social media accounts. Scammers have perpetrated confidence frauds since long before the internet, but computers and social media make them easier to carry out—and to do so from anywhere in the world.

Online Shopping Fraud

Online shopping fraud is another common type of scam. Frank Todd was one of its victims. Todd had not planned to buy a puppy online, he explained to the *Wall Street Journal*. He tried local breeders, but the supply had dried up. Everyone it seemed wanted a pet with which to ride out the COVID-19 pandemic. Then Todd saw a photo of Pippa online. The short-haired dachshund captured his heart. Todd exchanged emails with the seller, and using a mobile app, he paid $800 for the puppy. Pippa never came. Todd eventually figured out it was a fraud, but he still wonders, "Who scams with puppies?"[9]

In 2020, 38 percent of scams reported to the BBB were online shopping scams. Scammers lure victims with the promise of a bargain or hard-to-find items. Some create fake websites or social media ads that resemble trusted brands. Others post on legitimate sites like Amazon or eBay. Sometimes consumers suspect the bargain is too good to be true but take a chance anyway. Victims receive lower-quality goods or none at all.

Shoppers duped by online fraud typically incur minimal losses relative to other scams. The BBB reported a median loss of ninety-six dollars in 2020. But shopping scams do not cost just consumers. Retailers spend time and resources fighting fraudsters that steal photos of their products and sell counterfeits. According to the *Washington Post*, the clothing company Canada Goose closed down thirty thousand fake ads and websites in 2019. Amazon employs more than five thousand people to fight fraud. The time and money retailers spend dealing with online shopping fraud can impact their profits.

Identity Fraud

Identity fraud, another type of popular scam, comes in many forms including a SIM swap. In a SIM swap, a thief convinces or bribes a

Romance Fraud Victimizes More than Just the Target

The soldier's straight posture, forthright gaze, and decorated uniform suggested he was a man of strength and integrity. That is exactly why a scammer stole his photo, slapped on false contact information, and posted it to a dating website. In stealing the images of real soldiers, romance scammers harm more than just the people they target.

Former marine Daniel Anonsen knows all about the fallout from romance frauds. He has reported an estimated two hundred accounts to Facebook that use his image. In an interview with the *New York Times*, Anonsen says he has received desperate messages from women he does not actually know and even lost a girlfriend who grew suspicious of the online activity. For more than eleven years, US representative Adam Kinzinger has also battled scammers who use his photographs. Kinzinger served in the US Air Force and now serves in the Air National Guard. In 2015 a woman used all her savings to fly from India to meet him, believing they were in a relationship. Anonsen, Kinzinger, and others like them spend time, energy, and emotional capital dealing with the misuse of their photos.

phone carrier representative to switch a mobile number to a new SIM card. The scammers can then request new passwords for the victim's email, social media, and financial accounts. When password reset links or verification codes are sent as text messages, they go straight to the scammers. The scammers lock the victim out of their accounts and take control. SIM swap scammers often seek out targets with cryptocurrency accounts because cryptocurrency transactions are difficult to trace and reverse.

Twenty-one-year-old Joel Ortiz pleaded no contest in 2019 to stealing over $7.5 million from at least forty victims using a SIM swap. One of Ortiz's victims, technology consultant Seth Shapiro, lost his life savings in the SIM swap. Shapiro describes the moment he realized his cryptocurrency account had been drained of almost $2 million. "That was probably the worst moment of my life. I just sat there . . . helpless, knowing that everything we had was gone,"[10] he says. Shapiro's wife agrees. "It's been very hard on the kids. It's been very hard on our marriage. There's been many times where we didn't know if we were going to make it,"[11] she says. While Shapiro and his wife struggled to hold their fam-

A SIM swap is a type of fraud in which a thief convinces a phone company employee to switch a customer's mobile phone number to a new SIM card.

The video shows about two dozen workstations separated by plexiglass and stretching from one side of the gray-carpeted room to another. Agents outfitted with headsets sit in front of computers, taking calls from the United States, the United Kingdom, and Australia. They read from prepared scripts and enter information into a customer database. Supervisors monitor the activity and make reports to upper management. From the large whiteboard to the bland decor, this operation looks like a legitimate call center. But its business is tech-support scams. They begin with a computer pop-up or voicemail informing targets that malware has infected their computer. When targets call the number provided, the scammer offers to "fix" the computer for a fee.

Jim Browning (an alias) leaked the video footage of this Indian scam center. He hacked into its security cameras and voice data and then exposed the operation on his YouTube channel. The footage is disturbing. In smooth, authoritative voices, the scammers walk frazzled victims through the "recovery" process while stealing their money. The scammers snicker at the most distressed callers. Browning estimates this center made about $3 million a year.

ily together, Ortiz lived large. He dressed in Gucci clothing and, according to law enforcement, carried wads of cash, dropped $10,000 at Los Angeles clubs some nights, and spent $150,000 on a monthlong Airbnb rental.

Identity frauds come in different varieties. In e-skimming, for example, scammers hack into an online store and place malware on the retailer's checkout page. When customers enter their financial information, the scammers collect it too. Phishing emails appear to come from legitimate sources such as a bank or internet provider and attempt to trick targets into providing personal data. Phishing is often a first step in other scams or even sophisticated cyberattacks. SIM swaps, e-skimming, and phishing did not exist before the internet. They rely on cybertechnology.

Cyberscam Strategies

Frauds vary in their complexity, types of victims, technological sophistication, and impacts, but according to researchers Button and Cross, scammers use similar strategies to perpetrate them. First, scammers often invoke authority and legitimacy. In a shopping scam, for example, they might mimic the look of a legitimate retailer. In a tech-support fraud, they might use technical language when speaking to targets. Second, scammers often ask for small amounts of money, at least at first. Doing so can raise fewer suspicions among targets and less interest among authorities. Third, fraudsters appeal to targets' emotions. They know people fall more easily for a fake relationship when they are lonely or an employment scam when they are desperate for a job. Scammers get targets excited about a bargain or investment opportunity. They ask questions to provoke emotional responses, knowing that logic may falter when emotions run high. Fourth, scammers apply pressure by making frequent contact or imposing deadlines. In a grandparent scam, for example, a fraudster pretends to be a desperate grandchild in trouble. The money is needed urgently, the fraudster presses. The grandparent has no time to check the story. Fifth, scammers maintain physical distance from a victim. It is a hedge against empathy, according to Button and Cross, and practical for avoiding angry victims. Knowing the strategies, not just the kinds of scams, helps targets identify fraud in its various disguises.

Scammers use other strategies to avoid detection. Cybertechnology enables scammers to operate from locations with weak police enforcement. They typically request payment in gift cards, by wire, or in cryptocurrency, which make transactions difficult to trace or reverse. To make reporting less likely, scammers ask for small sums of money or make victims feel embarrassed to discuss the scam. Button and colleagues call some successful fraudsters "scampreneurs" because of the skill required in planning, perpetrating, and concealing their work. Successful scammers know how to match different types of fraud with different kinds of victims. Cybertechnology has enabled them to do so more efficiently and effectively.

Chapter Two

Ransomware Attacks

Anxiety simmered inside the cars wrapped around gas stations and snaked down roads. In early May 2021 a seemingly endless queue of drivers lined up across the Southeast for a dwindling supply of fuel. While they waited, drivers calculated distances and gas mileage. Would they have enough gas to go to work? Which errands could they skip? How long would the gas shortage last? When the gas ran out, people had little reason to stop in the convenience stores at gas stations for a forgotten necessity or a snack. Revenues, not just gas supplies, were drying up. Hurricanes and floods had choked the regional economy before, but this was no act of nature. This was a ransomware attack.

Days before the major gas shortages, an employee had discovered a ransom note on Colonial Pipeline's computer network. The company provides almost half of the East Coast's fuel. It carries gasoline, diesel, jet fuel, and home heating oil to communities extending from Texas, across the Southeast, and up to New York. Criminal hackers had breached Colonial Pipeline's network, encrypted the company's data, and stolen almost six thousand personal records, mostly of employees and their family members. The ransomware froze Colonial Pipeline's business operations. To contain the attack, the company shut down all 5,500 miles (8,851 km) of its pipeline. The ransomware

In May 2021 a ransomware attack against Colonial Pipeline forced the company to shut down its lines, resulting in fuel shortages from Texas to New York.

developers, later identified as the Russia-linked group DarkSide, demanded millions of dollars in Bitcoin to unlock the files.

The pipeline shutdown and ensuing panic led to severe gas shortages and price increases across the Southeast. Governors in five states declared a state of emergency. The US Department of Transportation declared a federal emergency for the region. American Airlines rerouted flights, and some military bases in the affected areas limited gasoline consumption. Biden urged Americans to remain calm, and the White House called Russia to discuss dismantling ransomware networks.

Colonial Pipeline paid the Bitcoin ransom, worth about $4.4 million, but it still took nearly a week to restart the pipeline. Turning on a pipeline, as Biden said, "is not like flicking on a light switch."[12] A week after the cyberattack, 72 percent of stations in North Carolina and 88 percent in Washington, DC, were out of gas, according to the real-time fuel price app GasBuddy. In some areas, gas supplies did not recover for another week or more. "As far as I know, this is the first cybersecurity incident that has led to a measurable economic impact on the American population,"[13] says cybersecurity expert Jonathan Reiber. A cyberattack on one company had hit the pocketbooks of consumers and gas station owners in an entire region.

Ransomware Attacks Surge

A volley of headline-grabbing ransomware attacks landed in the spring and summer of 2021. Just one month after the Colonial Pipeline hack, REvil extorted an $11 million ransom from JBS, a global meat supplier. One month later REvil demanded $70 million in the Kaseya ransomware attack. While these high ransom demands are unusual, ransomware attacks are not. In 2020 the FBI received almost twenty-five hundred ransomware complaints. Most cyberexperts, including those in the FBI, believe many attacks go unreported. Companies may fear that reporting an attack will tarnish their brand or make them look like easy prey. Cybersecurity firm SonicWall estimates that in 2020 there were actually more than 300 million ransomware attacks worldwide. "The number of these hacks and the scale of them is wildly out of control," says cybersecurity expert Matt Tait. It "is impacting ordinary folks' lives in a way that is very upsetting."[14]

Whatever the true number of ransomware attacks, it is growing. From 2019 to 2020, global ransomware attacks increased 62 percent, according to SonicWall. Ransom payments are also increasing. Over the same period, the average ransom payment rose 171 percent to $312,493, according to Palo Alto Networks.

Ransomware attacks on large companies with high ransoms grab big attention, but most ransomware attacks target small and midsize companies. Veterinarian offices, law firms, local libraries, and even individuals have all suffered. In 2020 ransomware attacks also impacted American cities, schools, and health care facilities. While the targets and the stakes vary, ransomware attacks follow a similar script.

> "The number of these hacks and the scale of them is wildly out of control. . . . [It] is impacting ordinary folks' lives in a way that is very upsetting."[14]
>
> —Matt Tait, cybersecurity expert

The FBI generally discourages but does not prohibit companies from paying ransoms. Benjamin Wittes and Alvaro Marañon, both from the Lawfare Institute, argue for a stricter policy. They believe ransom payments should be banned, with a few exceptions. They explain:

> Most ransomware victim companies or entities are not innocent victims. . . . They've left systems vulnerable. . . . Whenever one of these companies pays a ransom, they are effectively encouraging future attacks. They're feeding a marketplace. Unlike human ransoms where the cost is human life, in most of these situations, the cost is data, which may be catastrophic for the [affected] entity but is not catastrophic for the society. . . .
>
> [Companies] should be generally prohibited from making these payments with the exception of circumstances in which they apply for and receive permission from federal authorities to do so. Federal authorities should review those applications with an eye toward larger public policy considerations like is there an imminent loss of human life at issue, is there going to be catastrophic damage to the economy generally rather than simply to a company that failed to do cybersecurity due diligence.

Quoted in Scott R. Anderson, "How Can Congress Take on the Ransomware Problem?," August 16, 2021, in *Lawfare Podcast*, produced by Jen Patja Howell, podcast. www.lawfareblog.com.

The Hack

To launch ransomware, hackers need to breach the network of an organization or individual. Joseph Blount, chief executive officer (CEO) of Colonial Pipeline, testified in a Senate hearing that he believes hackers used a compromised password to access the Colonial Pipeline computer system through an old virtual private network (VPN). The VPN used single-factor authentication, which only requires a username and password for access. How the hackers got the password in the Colonial Pipeline breach is unknown. In some cases, hackers simply guess a password. This "brute-force" method sometimes involves remarkably little brute force. According to a 2019 Google/Harris poll, almost

Ransomware Payments Should Not Be Banned

Jen Ellis, a vice president at cybersecurity firm Rapid7, argues that banning ransomware payments will harm the most vulnerable organizations. She told the BBC:

> Banning payments would almost certainly result in a pretty horrific game of "chicken," whereby criminals would shift all their focus towards organizations which are least likely to be able to deal with downtime—for example hospitals, water-treatment plants, energy providers, and schools. The hackers may expect the harm to society caused by this downtime to apply the necessary pressure to ensure they get paid. They have very little to lose by doing this—and potentially a big payday to gain. Let's say the government creates a fund to support these organizations so they don't have to pay. If that happens, the attackers could then just switch their focus to small businesses and non-profit organizations which don't have the resources to protect themselves. They could face complete ruin if they don't pay. . . . Prohibiting payments is a great goal to shoot for. But we must be pragmatic in our approach to ensure we do not create significant economic and societal harm.

Quoted in Joe Tidy, "Ransomware: Should Paying Hacker Ransoms Be Illegal?," BBC, May 20, 2021. www.bbc.com.

one-quarter of Americans have used a password as simple as *123456* or *iloveyou*. In the case of Colonial Pipeline, however, Blount testified, "It was a complicated password. . . . It was not a 'colonial123'-type password."[15]

A Colonial Pipeline employee could have instead fallen victim to phishing. Ransomware attacks commonly begin with emails or texts sent to a wide pool of targets (phishing) or a specific target (spear phishing). Phishing can dupe users into divulging log-in credentials—usernames and passwords—or clicking a link or attachment that deploys malware on a computer. Phishing scams can be sophisticated. Attackers can research a target to personalize emails with the names of colleagues, company-specific acronyms, or visuals like logos or photos that add credibility to emails or fake log-in pages. Compromising passwords is not the only method of deploying ransomware. Hackers can also breach a network through software vulnerabilities or with previously stolen credentials.

Before launching ransomware, some attackers snoop around the breached network. Documents like financial statements or cyberinsurance policies stored on company servers can help the criminals determine how much ransom to demand. Hackers may also seek out confidential documents or personal data to sell. The threat of releasing the sensitive information can further pressure companies to pay the ransom. In some cases, hackers find and delete backups to give organizations even more reason to pay the ransom. When hackers finally deploy ransomware, it encrypts the files on a computer network so they become unusable. A ransom note appears on a computer informing the company it has been the victim of a ransomware attack and giving instructions about how to pay the ransom. The attackers usually demand cryptocurrency in return for a decryptor.

Ransomware attacks often start with a phishing scam in which a company's workers are sent emails that lure them into revealing log-in credentials for their employer's computer network.

The Hackers

Not all criminals have the technical expertise to develop ransomware, hack into a computer system, launch an attack, and steal data. Criminals without the necessary skills can turn to other criminal actors like an initial access broker (IAB) or ransomware-as-a-service (RaaS) group. IABs obtain and then sell access to a computer network. According to cybersecurity firm KELA, network access costs $5,400 on average but varies with the size of company and the level of access. RaaS groups, like DarkSide and REvil, write the ransomware programs. Affiliates identify a target, breach the target's computer network with or without the use of an IAB, and then use the developed RaaS ransomware to execute an attack. Affiliates and the RaaS group both take a cut of the ransom proceeds. According to the security firm FireEye, in 2021 DarkSide advertised taking a 25 percent cut of ransoms up to $500,000, with a smaller cut as the ransom amount increases.

When *New York Times* investigative reporter Michael Schwirtz got access to DarkSide's operations, what struck him most was "how mundane it is. It was like entering into any other company's computer systems." Some RaaS issue press releases, advertise their services on dark web forums, provide training to affiliates, have revenue goals, and offer customer service help lines for affiliates and victims. "It's the goal of these hackers," Schwirtz explains, "to make this as simple as possible so that people are more willing to just pay the ransom and . . . get back to business rather than put up a real fight."[16]

Finding and prosecuting ransomware criminals has proved difficult, in part because of countries that provide them safe havens. Some in the US government and cybersecurity experts

"It's the goal of these hackers to make this as simple as possible so that people are more willing to just pay the ransom and . . . get back to business rather than put up a real fight."[16]

—Michael Schwirtz, *New York Times* investigative reporter

believe that Russia could crack down on ransomware criminals but chooses not to. In return, the cybercriminal groups appear to avoid targeting Russian interests. According to one expert, at least some of the ransomware written by Russian-based groups has code to prevent it installing on computer systems that use the Russian language or have Russian IP addresses.

The Response

When the city of Atlanta, Georgia, was hit with a ransomware attack in March 2018, Mayor Keisha Lance Bottoms needed to respond to the "hostage situation,"[17] as she called it. The Iranian hackers SamSam had seized the city's computer system and were demanding a Bitcoin ransom worth about $51,000 for its release. Ransomware hit five of the city's thirteen departments. Police had to write reports by hand, courts could not validate warrants, and residents were unable to pay water bills. The hackers seemed to taunt city employees by changing the names of their encrypted files to "I'm sorry." Perhaps the attackers really did feel sorry in the end when Atlanta decided not to pay. For some services, the city temporarily adopted manual work-arounds. Some data were permanently lost. But a year after the attack, an attorney for the city said Atlanta had recovered and now has better cybersecurity.

> "We are dealing with a hostage situation."[17]
>
> —Keisha Lance Bottoms, mayor of Atlanta, Georgia

Lake City, Florida, also suffered a ransomware attack, but the city decided to pay. In June 2019 ransomware disabled the small city's computers, phones, and even copy machines. The cyberattack forced employees to conduct all business in person, and residents could only use cash to pay water and gas bills. The city had kept backup files, but they were stored on the same network as the originals. So the attack encrypted them too. In the end the city and its insurer paid the ransom of 42 Bitcoins, worth about $460,000 at the time.

In March 2018 Atlanta mayor Keisha Lance Bottoms referred to a ransomware attack, in which hackers demanded $51,000 to release the city's computer system, as a "hostage situation."

When deciding whether to pay a ransom, victims wrestle with technological, financial, and practical considerations. They assess the extent of the ransomware's impact. Have the attackers taken confidential data? Does the organization have usable backups to restore data? Victims also weigh the costs of lost revenue and downtime against the ransom demand. Some organizations, like Lake City, have insurance to cover most of the ransom, which can make the decision to pay easier. Even after the financial and practical considerations, ransomware victims must consider the larger implications of payment. Paying a ransom, the FBI and others contend, can encourage future attacks and fund other illegal activities. It also does not guarantee the attackers will provide a useful decryptor or any decryptor at all. Although the details of their deliberations are not public, Atlanta and Lake City weighed these and other factors and came to opposite decisions.

The Aftermath

Whether or not a victim pays the ransom, recovery is not easy or cheap. "Coming back online can be like walking into your home after being robbed. Files aren't where they used to be and software doesn't always work right,"[18] writes cybersecurity reporter Kartikay Mehrotra. After paying the ransom, Lake City received a decryptor, but decrypting files took a lot of computer resources. Almost a month after the attack, many of the city's files remained locked. Costs of an attack to the victim include restoration, increased security, and lost revenue. Atlanta mayor Bottoms testified to Congress in June 2019 that the city, which did not pay the $51,000 ransom, had spent $7.2 million recovering from the attack so far.

While victims of ransomware attacks confront big costs, perpetrators rarely face any. The countries from which they operate often allow the criminals to act with impunity. Because cryptocurrency is hard to trace, the criminals are also less likely to face consequences. Occasionally, it works out differently. One month after the Colonial Pipeline attack, the US Department of Justice announced it had recovered most of the ransom. It provided no details on how it did so.

Gas supplies have recovered, but the cyberattack on Colonial Pipeline left its mark on the minds of CEOs and the agendas of policy makers. An attack on critical infrastructure like a fuel pipeline, electric grid, or transportation system does not just have the potential to hurt the economy. It could also threaten national security. Mark Montgomery, executive director of the Cyberspace Solarium Commission, thinks Americans got lucky this time.

Chapter Three

Nation-State Attacks

FireEye gets paid to be suspicious. So in December 2020, when the cybersecurity firm saw someone log in to its computer system with an expected username and password but a new phone number, staff reached out. The employee associated with the questionable log in said he did not have a new number. An icy wave of realization soaked the staff. If the employee did not have a new number, then the person with the new number had the employee's password. The FireEye network had been breached. "We didn't know a lot at the time," FireEye CEO Kevin Mandia says. "It just felt like it was time to brace for impact."[19] FireEye tore into its network to figure out who was in, where they had come from, and what they knew.

FireEye had discovered an enormous supply chain cyberattack. Such attacks penetrate a network by compromising software or hardware that a target uses. In this case, hackers embedded malicious code into a routine update of a business software made by SolarWinds. When business customers installed the update, as FireEye did, they unknowingly opened the door for malware to crawl onto their computer networks. About eighteen thousand customers downloaded the update. The attackers did not infiltrate all of them. But hackers carefully trod through the networks of some of SolarWinds' customers for up to nine months. Using the SolarWinds update and

other attack vectors, the hackers hit dozens of companies and nine government agencies. Victims included Microsoft, Cisco, Intel, thirty-seven defense companies, the US Department of the Treasury, the US Department of Homeland Security, and the US Department of Justice.

Few hackers have the skill required to conduct a supply chain attack and remain undetected for months in the systems of technologically sophisticated organizations. Analysts and the US government believe Russia most likely pulled it off. Threat analysts specifically suspect Cozy Bear, a hacker group within Russia's Foreign Intelligence Service. Presumably, the operation collected intelligence. Some wonder whether hackers have also left back doors to use for a different kind of operation in the future.

The Fifth Domain

The US Department of Defense calls cyberspace the fifth domain after land, sea, air, and space. Nation-states conduct operations and vie for power within cyberspace just as they do in the other domains. Cybertools empower nation-states to conduct traditional activities, like espionage, on a much greater scale. They also enable new kinds of weapons and warfare. Whether for espionage or sabotage, some of the most sophisticated cyberattacks depend on software flaws to deliver malware.

The Council on Foreign Relations suspects that thirty-four countries have conducted cyberattacks since 2005. Russia, Iran, China, and North Korea account for over three-quarters of the suspected operations. But it was the United States that opened the door to the fifth domain. In 2007 Iran was hurtling toward nuclear armament faster than anyone had expected. Israel requested American help to stop the advance. President George W. Bush examined his options. Diplomacy had not worked so far. Air strikes or another conventional military action could escalate tensions into a war that the United States did not want to trigger. Soon General Keith Alexander, then director of the National Security Agency (NSA), brought Bush a third option. In the past the United States had collected intelligence about Iran's nuclear program. Now it plotted a hack to sabotage it. The United States and Israel developed a cyberweapon known as Stuxnet.

Details of Stuxnet remain classified, but researchers believe it debuted in 2009 or 2010. Stuxnet likely jumped off a USB drive onto a single computer in Natanz, an Iranian nuclear facility. Exploiting multiple software flaws, Stuxnet crept through Natanz's computer network, dodging security defenses along the way. When it found its target, centrifuges whirling like tornadoes, it dropped its payload. In its final version, Stuxnet spun the centrifuges alternately too fast or too slow, damaging the uranium enrichment process. To remain undetected, Stuxnet replaced the actual data in the monitoring system with prerecorded data, just like in a Hollywood heist.

Over time, as more and more centrifuges wobbled and failed, Iran must have suspected sabotage. There was no proof until the worm escaped. In the summer of 2010, Stuxnet zigzagged its way around the world. When cyberanalysts caught and dissected its code, they discovered "one of the most sophisticated attack tools ever,"[20] as cybersecurity experts Richard A. Clarke and Robert K. Knake characterize it. Only a nation-state with deep cyberexpertise could have created it. Stuxnet demonstrated that cyberweapons could inflict real-world damage, and no one would forget it.

Researchers believe that in 2009 or 2010, agents for the United States and Israel used a cyberweapon called Stuxnet to disable centrifuges at the Iranian nuclear facility Natanz, pictured in 2019.

The United States tops the Belfer Center's ranking of countries with the greatest cyberpower, but conventional military strength is not a prerequisite for making the list. Iran and the Netherlands rank among the ten countries with the greatest cyberoffense, and Estonia ranks eleventh. Developing and launching cyberattacks can cost far less than traditional weapons and operations. "The barrier to entry to having a meaningful cyber-war offensive force is low," Clarke and Knake warn. "Countries that could never defeat the United States in a purely conventional military battle can pose significant asymmetric risks to us in cyberspace."[21] Cyberspace could rebalance the distribution of global powers by making espionage and sabotage more efficient and effective.

Espionage in Cyberspace

All nations spy, and they always have. Perhaps that is why some American officials seemed unfazed, although not unconcerned, when they discovered in 2015 that hackers, widely suspected to work for the Chinese government, had breached the US Office of Personnel Management (OPM). "You have to kind of salute the Chinese for what they did. If we had the opportunity to do that, I don't think we'd hesitate for a minute,"[22] says James Clapper, former director of national intelligence. Intelligence helps policy makers and military leaders make informed decisions about threats. Despite public denunciations, nation-states largely expect and accept espionage as part of international relations.

Some wonder though whether the speed and reach of intelligence gathering in cyberspace requires new norms. In the OPM attack, Chinese hackers stole employment or security-clearance records for more than 22 million people in less than eighteen months. Compare that, the *Economist* suggests, to a highly successful espionage foray in decades past. It took Vasili Mitrokhin twelve years starting in 1972 to smuggle twenty-five thousand pages out of the Soviet Union's spy agency archives. It took another eight years to deliver the information to British intelligence. Cyberspace has turbocharged the collection of intelligence by making it easier and faster.

> "The barrier to entry to having a meaningful cyber-war offensive force is low. Countries that could never defeat the United States in a purely conventional military battle can pose significant asymmetric risks to us in cyberspace."[21]
>
> —Richard A. Clarke and Robert K. Knake, experts in cybersecurity policy

Information on American government policies and investigations may have been a main goal in the SolarWinds attack. But cyberspies also target the private sector to steal intellectual property. Intellectual property is the ideas, technologies, and designs that individuals or organizations invent. In the past, state-sponsored hackers in China, Russia, and Iran have breached American companies, research institutions, and universities. In March 2016, for example, Chinese national Su Bin pleaded guilty to hacking private defense contractors. Bin stole information about the American F-22 and F-35 fighter jets and then passed it to the Chinese government. Defense experts say the origami-like folds and pencil-sharp nose of China's J-20 compared to the F-22 leave little doubt that China copied the jet's exterior design. More recently, the United States has accused Russia and China of hacking into the computers of COVID-19 vaccine researchers. Instead of developing technology or pharmaceuticals from scratch, companies that benefit from state-sponsored intellectual property theft start laps ahead. The Belfer Center estimates that China's cybertheft of intellectual property costs the United States $300 billion a year. The scope, space, and cost of cyberespionage differentiates it from traditional espionage.

Sabotage from Cyberspace

While most nation-state cyberattacks stop at intelligence gathering, others cause disruption and destruction. The costliest cyberattack to date is NotPetya. In a nondescript office building set among treeless roads and chunky, industrial buildings, a small Ukrainian software company was carrying out its daily routines in the spring of 2017. To-do lists got made, bills sent and paid, and bugs patched. That is, until Russian operatives slipped malicious code onto the server running the company's M.E.Doc tax accounting software.

On June 27, 2017, Russian government hackers unleashed NotPetya strapped to an M.E.Doc software update. The malware spread to the thousands of computers running the accounting software. No decryption key could bring back the data NotPetya wiped from the computers it attacked. Its goal was destruction, not criminal profit or even espionage. NotPetya rocketed through Ukraine. According to technology journalist Andy Greenberg, the malware obliterated a large Ukrainian bank network in just forty-five seconds and part of a major transit hub network in sixteen seconds. By the end of the day, the malware had taken down airports, gas pumps, bus stations, railroads, power companies, banks, most of the postal system, hospitals, ATMs, and almost all of the federal government. Ukrainian information technology (IT) administrator Pavlo Bondarenko told Greenberg, "Life went very fast from 'What's new on Face-

In March 2016, a Chinese national named Su Bin hacked private defense contractors and stole information about the new American F-22 (pictured) and F-35 fighter jets.

book?' to 'Do I have enough money to buy food for tomorrow?'"[23] The worm arrived just in time to commemorate Ukraine's independence day. The timing was no coincidence. Russia intended to demonstrate control over its neighbor to the west.

Computer worms, however, pay no attention to national borders. Cranes loading and unloading goods from ships froze across the globe when NotPetya infected computers at Maersk, a giant shipping operator. Maersk suffered an estimated $300 million loss from the attack. NotPetya halted vaccine production at the pharmaceutical company Merck, and doctors at hospitals in parts

> "Life went very fast from 'What's new on Facebook?' to 'Do I have enough money to buy food for tomorrow?'"[23]
>
> —Pavlo Bondaronko, Ukrainian IT administrator

of Virginia and Pennsylvania could not access patient records. NotPetya hit snack company Mondelez, shutting down machines at its Cadbury chocolate factory in Tasmania and disrupting its supply chain. Six weeks after NotPetya's launch, FedEx's European operations had still not completely recovered. In total, NotPetya caused an estimated loss of $10 billion or more. In the end, insurers for Merck and Mondelez refused to pay out, saying the event was an

33

The US Government Should Disclose Zero-Days to American Companies

Brad Smith, president of Microsoft, thinks the federal government should alert companies about zero-days instead of keeping them secret. Following the WannaCry ransomware attack in May 2017, he wrote:

> This attack provides yet another example of why the stockpiling of vulnerabilities by governments is such a problem. . . . Repeatedly, exploits in the hands of governments have leaked into the public domain and caused widespread damage. . . .
>
> The governments of the world should treat this attack as a wake-up call. They need to take a different approach and adhere in cyberspace to the same rules applied to weapons in the physical world. We need governments to consider the damage to civilians that comes from hoarding these vulnerabilities and the use of these exploits. This is one reason we called in February for a new "Digital Geneva Convention" to govern these issues, including a new requirement for governments to report vulnerabilities to vendors, rather than stockpile, sell, or exploit them. And it's why we've pledged our support for defending every customer everywhere in the face of cyberattacks, regardless of their nationality.

Brad Smith, "The Need for Urgent Collective Action to Keep People Safe Online: Lessons from Last Week's Cyberattack," *Microsoft on the Issues* (blog), Microsoft, May 14, 2017. https://blogs .microsoft.com.

act of war and therefore not covered by insurance. No doubt remains about the amount of destruction a cyberweapon can deliver.

Nation-states can use cybertools to harm more than just computer networks and businesses. They can harm political processes. During the 2016 American presidential election, Fancy Bear, a group within Russian intelligence, hacked the Democratic National Committee and Hillary Clinton's campaign. Russian intelligence posted thousands of the hacked emails and documents online. Russian government operatives also hacked into American state voter registration rolls and pretended to be Americans on social media to distribute misinformation, sow discord, and discourage voting. Collecting information on foreign political campaigns is

The US Government Should Not Disclose Zero-Days to American Companies

According to Rick Ledgett, former deputy director of the NSA, the US government already discloses a vast number of vulnerabilities. Ledgett thinks disclosing all vulnerabilities could harm Americans and US interests. He writes:

> Such disclosure would be tantamount to unilateral disarmament in an area where the U.S. cannot afford to be unarmed. Computer network exploitation tools are used every day to protect U.S. and allied forces in war zones, to identify threats to Americans overseas, and to isolate and disrupt terrorist plots directed against our homeland and other nations. It is no exaggeration to say that giving up those capabilities would cost lives. And this is not an area in which American leadership would cause other countries to change what they do. Neither our allies nor our adversaries would give away the vulnerabilities in their possession, and our doing so would probably cause those allies to seriously question our ability to be trusted with sensitive sources and methods.

Rick Ledgett, "No, the U.S. Government Should Not Disclose All Vulnerabilities in Its Possession," *Lawfare* (blog), August 7, 2017. www.lawfareblog.oom.

VIEWPOINTS

common, but as national security reporters Ellen Nakashima and Shane Harris say, "using digital tools to steal data and then release it to embarrass and stoke divisions—weaponizing information—was the innovation."[24] During the 2020 presidential campaign, Russia tried similar tactics.

There is no evidence that Russia or any other nation-state directly impacted vote tallies in either the 2016 or 2020 presidential election. Nevertheless, Russian actions may have undermined confidence in the election system and amplified divisions within American society. Cyberspace enables nation-states to gather intelligence at supersonic speeds and inflict harm on countries in ways that could not have been imagined before the internet.

Zero-Days

Kaseya, Stuxnet, and other highly sophisticated cyberattacks used zero-days to deliver malware. A zero-day is a previously unknown flaw in a piece of software or hardware. Modern software contains millions of lines of code. The F-35 fighter jet, for example, has at least 8 million lines of code. The software for Facebook consists of an estimated 61 million lines. That offers lots of opportunity for human coders to make mistakes or inadvertently leave vulnerabilities. When developers become aware of vulnerabilities, they create and issue patches, but the process can take time. Even after a patch becomes available, not everyone updates his or her software promptly. Some cyberattacks, like NotPetya, rely instead on known vulnerabilities that targets have not yet patched.

There is a market for zero-days, which cybersecurity writer Nicole Perlroth has researched extensively. Hackers working for governments, for companies, or as freelancers discover zero-days. Governments, software developers, and occasionally criminal organizations buy zero-days. According to Perlroth, a zero-day that can breach an iPhone's iOS software remotely would fetch $2.5 million or more.

The United States is among the nation-states that have collected zero-days or cybertools based on zero-days to use in cyberattacks. Instead of alerting the developers, including American ones, about the zero-days, the United States has in some cases held on to them to use in cyberattacks. In 2016 a group calling itself the Shadow Brokers started dumping NSA exploits online. No one knows how the Shadow Brokers obtained the exploits, but the implications were obvious. "It effectively puts cyber weapons in the hands of anyone who downloads it,"[25] says cybersecurity expert Matthew Hickey. One of the leaked exploits, EternalBlue, was later used in NotPetya and other cyberattacks, although it was not technically a zero-day exploit by then. Unlike traditional weapons, cyberweapons can be leaked and reused by adversaries. Cyberspace has changed the nature of espionage and sabotage.

Chapter Four

Defending Against Scams and Attacks

It took just fifteen seconds for the first bank employee to fall for Sherri Davidoff's phishing scam. After one minute, seventeen employees had clicked on a link that took them to a fake online survey. Davidoff had created the web page to trick employees into giving her their usernames and passwords. The web page looked authentic. Davidoff had used the same fonts, logo, and background colors as the actual bank website and pasted in headshots of bank management. With employee credentials, Davidoff could have clawed into the bank's network and tried to steal customers' financial data or plant ransomware. But Davidoff did not try. As biographer Jeremy Smith details, the bank had hired her to hack its network.

Penetration testers like Davidoff break into buildings and networks (with permission) to demonstrate the vulnerabilities of organizations before criminals or nation-state aggressors exploit them. They are part of a growing cybersecurity industry. As attackers have grown more sophisticated, so have defenders—the individuals and organizations trying to stop cyberscams and cyberattacks. Defenders try to discourage cyberaggressions by making these acts more costly and less lucrative and by enhancing tools for protection and response.

Strategies for Cybersecurity

It can seem like attackers always have the advantage over defenders, but that mind-set frustrated technology professional Rohan Amin and his colleagues. "We were tired of this victim mentality, woe-is-us, nothing-we-can-do, defeatist attitude,"[26] he says. So in 2011 Amin and his colleagues took a new perspective. They dissected an attack into a process. To succeed, an adversary typically researches a target, develops or acquires cybertools, accesses a network, establishes a line of communication, moves around, and carries out an objective such as stealing data, delivering ransomware, or sabotaging a system. Defenders deter attacks by making it harder for an attacker to succeed at each point in this process.

Many organizations serious about defense use a strategy based on the National Institute of Standards and Technology (NIST) cybersecurity framework. The framework organizes cybersecurity into five functions. The first function is to identify a network's assets and vulnerabilities. Over time, networks can become like sock drawers. Software and hardware get added and subtracted—and then those changes are forgotten. That leaves gaps for intruders to poke through. The Colonial Pipeline attacker, for example, came through a VPN that was "not intended to be in use,"[27] according to the CEO. Attackers will investigate every dusty corner of a target's network. Defenders need to know it even better.

Protecting the network, the framework's second function, focuses on preventing and mitigating breaches. Basic hygiene can discourage low-level attacks. Users need complicated passwords, and organizations should use multifactor authentication. This requires information from at least two of three categories: something you know (your password), something you have (like a texted code), and something you are (such as your fingerprint). Updating software also helps prevent breaches. NotPetya spread in part because of companies that had failed to install a Microsoft patch issued three months before the attack. More than two years after Microsoft released the update, almost 1 million computers still had not installed it. Protecting a network's perimeter also means safeguarding physical assets, such as server rooms and devices, and running antivirus software.

While important, basic hygiene will not stop a determined attacker. Organizations and individuals must protect more than their perimeter. Networks operating on the principle of zero trust limit a user's movements. Accessing the network should not mean accessing every sensitive document on the network. Employees should have as little access to files and applications as possible. Zero-trust networks also continuously verify a user's identity by monitoring behavior. A user who suddenly starts communicating with new people or accessing new areas of the network raises a red flag. For example, when cybersecurity professional Juan Roa Salinas saw a computer at the financial services firm where he worked look up an IP address in North Korea, he knew something was wrong. According to reporter Ed Caesar, Salinas was aware of North Korea's brazen attacks on financial institutions. Salinas took the company offline, which stopped the intruders before they

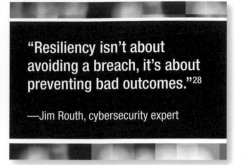

"Resiliency isn't about avoiding a breach, it's about preventing bad outcomes."[28]

—Jim Routh, cybersecurity expert

could complete their job. "Resiliency isn't about avoiding a breach, it's about preventing bad outcomes,"[28] says cybersecurity expert Jim Routh. Basic hygiene combined with a zero-trust approach reduces the likelihood of a cyberscam or cyberattack and limits an intruder's access to sensitive documents and functions.

Cyberattacks are inevitable. The third function in NIST's framework is to detect intruders before they can do damage. Serious defenders assume a breach has occurred and scour their systems for intruders. Intruders can hide inside a network for weeks or even months. NIST's fourth function is to develop a response in case of attack. An effective response plan details how to contain an attack, mitigate damage, and communicate about an incident. Effective response also involves understanding how an incident happened and its impact. The law does not typically require organizations to report a cyberattack, but sharing information can help stop attacks or prevent future ones. If FireEye had not voluntarily announced it was the victim of the SolarWinds attack, adversaries might have remained inside other networks much longer. Information sharing also raises the cost of launching a cyberattack because it makes it harder for attackers to reuse tools.

Recovering after an attack, the fifth function in the framework, entails removing the attacker, restoring data, rebuilding systems, and improving defenses. This process can take days to months, depending on the size of the organization, the type of malware used, the state of backups, and the experience of the recovery team. Multilayered, zero-trust protection makes attackers work harder to breach and remain in networks. Detecting and responding quickly to attacks can prevent attackers from accomplishing their objectives. The NIST framework provides individuals and organizations with a strategy to improve cybersecurity, but it is not the only approach.

Defending Forward

General Paul M. Nakasone, commander of US Cyber Command, thinks the best defense is a good offense. In 2018 US Cyber Command adopted a new strategy: defend forward and engage continuously with adversaries. Defending forward means proactively disrupting cyberattacks. Cyberpolicy expert Richard J. Harknett says, "Previous U.S. approaches ultimately left the U.S. playing 'clean-up on aisle nine,' too often dealing with adversaries inside our networks (or in the aftermath of their exploitations), rather than stopping them before entering."[29] Engaging continuously means not letting adversaries catch their breath.

In 2020 US Cyber Command disrupted the TrickBot botnet. TrickBot is a collection of computers, perhaps more than 1 million of them, that are believed to be controlled by Russian-speaking criminals. The botnet receives instructions from operators and has been used in the past to deliver ransomware and steal personal data. In September of that year, US Cyber Command hacked the TrickBot servers and severed the communication between infected computers around the world and the botnet's operators. It also injected false information into TrickBot's collection of stolen data.

Under the leadership of General Paul M. Nakasone, the US Cyber Command has adopted the strategy of proactively disrupting cyberattacks.

GEN Na

When the operators recovered the connection, US Cyber Command disrupted it again. Some speculate that US Cyber Command took action to protect the US presidential election process. The operation's purpose may also have been to protect against future ransomware or nation-state attacks.

TrickBot still operates today, but that does not necessarily mean the operation failed, especially if judged by the criteria of persistent engagement. "There's lots of ways in which it makes great sense to put the Trickbot operators through their paces repeatedly," says national security expert Robert Chesney, ". . . just to increase friction for adversaries and to make life harder, make them spend their resources on things other than causing trouble directly."[30] US Cyber Command believes proactive and continuous engagement with adversaries deters cyberattacks by raising their cost. The strategy can also position the US military for future actions.

The Defenders

Implementing a good defense strategy does not come cheap. Bank of America spends more than $1 billion per year on cybersecurity, and other large American banks spend a similar amount. Some of that money goes to buying products and some to paying penetration testers, bug hunters, and response teams. Penetration testers identify risks. They attempt to hack into networks and, depending on the engagement, may also try to physically access devices. Like scammers and attackers, penetration testers rely heavily on social engineering to trick employees into granting access or divulging information. They pretend to be frazzled new employees, busy inspectors, helpful maintenance workers, or anyone else who might need access to an office, server room, or a computer. These professionals help organizations improve their protection and detection functions.

Bug hunters provide another layer of defense by uncovering zero-days before attackers do. In the early days of computers, software developers ignored or threatened to sue hackers who reported vulnerabilities to them. Now they pay for that information.

Apple, Google, Microsoft, and many other technology firms have bug bounty programs that reward hackers for finding errors in their code. The most flagrant flaws earn the highest payouts. Over a three-month period in 2020, twenty-year-old Sam Curry and his team found fifty-five bugs in Apple's corporate network. Apple paid them almost $300,000. The US Department of Defense also sponsors bug bounty programs. In the first year of Hack the Pentagon, it took just thirteen minutes for hackers to identify the first vulnerability. A few bug hunters earn enough to make it a full-time job. Others do it to supplement their income or as a hobby. "You feel like a detective, going in rooting around and saying, 'That looks interesting,' and having a stream of clues," says bug bounty hunter Katie Paxton-Fear. "And, when you get all the pieces neatly together, and it works and there's a bug there—it's the most thrilling experience ever."[31] Like penetration testers, bug hunters identify risks to strengthen protection.

> "You feel like a detective, going in rooting around and saying, 'That looks interesting,' and having a stream of clues. And, when you get all the pieces neatly together, and it works and there's a bug there—it's the most thrilling experience ever."[31]
>
> —Katie Paxton-Fear, bug bounty hunter

The Defend Forward Policy Will Strengthen American Security

VIEWPOINTS

General Paul M. Nakasone, commander of US Cyber Command, director of the National Security Agency, and chief of the Central Security Service, believes rival nations are using cyberoperations to degrade American power. The defend forward strategy, he argues, is an appropriate response, consistent with the actions of "adversaries and competitors," to protect Americans and their interests.

We must "defend forward" in cyberspace, as we do in the physical domains. Our naval forces do not defend by staying in port, and our airpower does not remain at airfields. They patrol the seas and skies to ensure they are positioned to defend our country before our borders are crossed. The same logic applies in cyberspace. Persistent engagement of our adversaries in cyberspace cannot be successful if our actions are limited to DOD [US Department of Defense] networks. To defend critical military and national interests, our forces must operate against our enemies on their virtual territory as well. Shifting from a response outlook to a persistence force that defends forward moves our cyber capabilities out of their virtual garrisons, adopting a posture that matches the cyberspace operational environment.

Paul M. Nakasone, "A Cyber Force for Persistent Operations," *Joint Force Quarterly*, January 2019, p. 11.

If disaster strikes, an organization forms a response team. It could include outside cybersecurity experts and insurance representatives. Like many parts of the response process, ransomware negotiations can feel like a ticking time bomb. Professional negotiators can help. In online chats with criminals, negotiators attempt to lower ransom demands. They may also try to buy time to determine the usefulness of a company's backups. Negotiators work carefully with distressed clients and with criminals to keep the conversation going. "Sometimes you're negotiating in two directions at once—with the hacker and with the victim," says ransomware negotiator Kurtis Minder. "You have to . . . be empathetic but also give directions in a way that isn't confrontational."[32]

Incident response teams also track attackers, root them out, assess the damage, recover files and systems, and recommend

Brandon Valeriano and Benjamin Jensen, experts in cybersecurity and military strategy at Marine Corps University, believe that defending forward is a weak strategy with the potential to escalate international conflict. They write:

> The rationale behind persistent action—that the best defense is a good offense—is deeply flawed. In fact, most military and strategic theory holds that the defense is the superior posture. . . . The stronger form of war is a deception-driven defense: confusing an attacker so that they waste resources attacking strong points that appear weak. . . . Rather than persistent action and preemptive strikes on adversary networks, the United States needs persistent deception and defensive counterstrikes optimized to undermine adversary planning and capabilities. . . .
>
> Shifting to a policy of preemptive offensive cyberwarfare risks provoking fear and overreaction in other states and possibly producing conflict spirals. Even limited-objective cyber offensive action defined as "defending forward" can be misinterpreted and lead to inadvertent escalation.

Brandon Valeriano and Benjamin Jensen, "The Myth of the Cyber Offense: The Case for Restraint," *Policy Analysis*, January 15, 2019, pp. 6–7.

security improvements. When NotPetya crippled the computer networks of shipping giant Maersk, the company triaged the crisis from its offices in Maidenhead, England. Technology staff from around the world arrived to help. As many as 400 employees and more than 130 people from a consulting firm providing technical assistance worked in shifts to stitch the network and business back together. After four weeks, they had rebuilt over forty-five thousand laptops. The cybersecurity ecosystem includes professionals who work on every step of the defense process.

Recent Policy Responses

As important as cybersecurity professionals are, they alone cannot solve the problem. Policy makers have a unique role in cybersecurity. They can make new rules and levy consequences to fortify targets, punish attackers, and reduce collateral damage from attacks. The Biden administration has implemented several new measures. In May 2021 Biden issued an executive order to increase cybersecurity at federal agencies and the companies that sell technology to the federal government. Among other things, the order directs NIST to develop cybersecurity standards for suppliers, requires federal agencies to use multifactor authentication and principles of zero trust, and helps ensure that suppliers and agencies report cyberthreats and incidents. "It's the most ambitious cybersecurity effort from an administration in decades,"[33] says cybersecurity expert Ari Schwartz, who worked in the Barack Obama administration.

In 2021 the US Department of Homeland Security (DHS) issued two directives requiring operators of critical pipelines, including those that transport oil and natural gas, to improve their cybersecurity. Operators will need to implement specific security measures, develop contingency and recovery plans, and report threats and incidents. The DHS was also expected to issue cybersecurity mandates for the transportation industry. Improving the cybersecurity of critical infrastructure can help protect the public.

The White House also attempts to deter cyberattacks with foreign policy. In April 2021 the United States imposed sanctions on Russia for activities that included election meddling and the SolarWinds attack. Three months later the United States and its allies publicly accused China of cyberespionage.

As cyberattacks have become more sophisticated, so have some defenders. The best implement sophisticated defense strategies with help from products and professionals. Yet many individuals and organizations have taken only minimal steps to secure their networks and assets. No matter how sophisticated a single organization's defense, if the electricity goes out, food or water supplies get poisoned, or an attacker slips malware into the supply chain, it may not matter. Deterring cyberscams and cyberattacks will require a more coordinated effort.

Chapter Five

What More Can Be Done?

US president Joe Biden and Russian president Vladimir Putin met in June 2021 in Geneva, Switzerland. It was just weeks after Russian criminals had carried out a ransomware attack on Colonial Pipeline. American officials do not believe the Russian government launched the attack, but some think Russia could arrest ransomware criminals if it wanted. At a press conference following the summit, a reporter asked Biden whether he had told Putin the consequences for damaging critical American infrastructure. Biden said, "I pointed out to him that we have significant cyber capability, and he knows it. . . . If in fact [Russians] violate these basic norms, we will respond . . . in the cyber way."[34] Two weeks later, a Russian-based group carried out the Kaseya ransomware attacks, demanding $70 million for a decryptor. Strong words alone, even from powerful people, have not stopped cyberscams or cyberattacks. What more can be done?

New technology might improve cybersecurity, but it will also benefit attackers. Better collaborations between the public and private sectors could harden targets, and international coordination may reduce criminal profits. Nation-states could also set ground rules for cyberspace. But in the end, the country may need a good backup plan.

When President Joe Biden met with Russian president Vladimir Putin in June 2021, Biden warned Putin that the United States would respond in kind to cyberattacks.

New Technologies for Better or Worse

Artificial intelligence empowers computers to do more than just take orders. Machine learning, one form of artificial intelligence, allows computers to learn by example or experience. Machine learning algorithms uncover patterns in large amounts of data and work faster and more effectively than humans on certain kinds of problems. Machine learning has been used in spam filters since the early 2000s. Today most machine learning applications in cybersecurity focus on the detection of spam, intruders, or malware. Other applications can identify and prioritize network vulnerabilities by comparing known threats with the software an organization runs. Machine learning also helps protect networks by authenticating users based on a complex set of factors, including, for example, geographic location and typing style. But current technologies leave room for improvement. Detection algorithms can produce many false positives, and few applications support response and recovery functions.

In their crystal ball, Micah Musser and Ashton Garriott from the Center for Security and Emerging Technology see new machine learning applications. Future technology could actively defend networks. Computers could generate fake documents, emails, or network data to confuse attackers, waste their time, convince them they have succeeded, or trick them into divulging information or downloading software. Computers may one day also collect and analyze information from the dark web about zero-days or other threats. Refinements in current machine learning applications and development of new ones will benefit defenders.

Advances in machine learning also have the potential to better arm the offense. Organizations can use the vulnerabilities that machine learning applications find to patch their defenses. Attackers could use the same information to select flaws for exploitation. Machine learning can generate realistic text, audio, and video, potentially making phishing or disinformation campaigns even more convincing. Impersonating a boss, client, or friend will become easier. Using machine learning requires expertise that large organizations and nation-states have and criminal organizations could acquire, if they have not done so already.

Machine learning presents challenges too. Most algorithms require large data sets to work effectively. They also consume significant computational resources, especially to work in complex environments. Quantum computing may be the revolution that machine learning needs to leap forward. When it is fully developed, quantum computing will allow computers to solve problems too complicated for today's computers. With quantum computing, machine learning applications could work in more complex environments.

Like machine learning, quantum computing is a double-edged sword. Cyberexperts Richard A. Clarke and Robert K. Knake call it the "magic decoder ring."[35] Web browsers, email, and ATMs, among other things, use encryption to protect data transfers. Today's encryption uses mathematical calculations that even a supercomputer could not reasonably reverse. But one day—perhaps a decade or more from now, quantum computers will crack today's un-decryptable messages. In response, governments, technology

ATMs use encryption to protect data transfers. Today's encryption uses mathematical calculations that even a supercomputer could not reasonably reverse.

leaders, and researchers are developing new kinds of encryption. Defenders must aggressively pursue new technologies just to keep up with attackers, but new technology will not end cyberscams and cyberattacks. What else can make a difference?

Public and Private Sectors Working Better Together

When it comes to cyberattacks, companies in the private sector are concerned with protecting their profits. Governments and other organizations in the public sector are concerned with protecting the public. While the public and private sectors may have somewhat different goals, they are bound together. Most critical infrastructure is owned and operated by the private sector. A cyberattack on a company in one of the sixteen critical infrastructure areas could hurt more than just profit. It could damage the economy, public health, or national security. Public entities like local governments, public schools, and police also run software and hardware made by American tech companies. Supply chain attacks that exploit a flaw in Google, Microsoft, or Apple could disrupt the functioning of the public sector and harm individuals. The public sector benefits from technological innovation, which is often driven by the private sector. By design, the United States separates public and private sectors, but the scope, scale, and targets of today's cyberattacks require better collaboration.

The public and private sectors have not always partnered well. Some business leaders have strongly opposed any government rules that could impact their operations. Some policy makers believe the recent increases in cyberattacks show that more government involvement is necessary. Recent policy efforts have focused on two areas: minimum security standards and information sharing across public and private sectors. To Chris Wysopal, chief technology officer at a cybersecurity firm, standards just make sense. "We have minimum standards for fire safety because there is collateral damage to adjacent structures from fires and limited public resources for fighting fires. We are now seeing the same risks coming to cybersecurity,"[36] he says. The federal government could require or create incentives for organizations to implement multifactor authentication, encryption, software patching, more rigorous testing of new software, or other security standards. Biden and the DHS took the first steps in 2021 when they required owners and operators of critical pipelines and federal agencies to adopt minimum standards. But many other critical infrastructure operators and organizations have no such standards. A 2021 *Washington Post* survey of cybersecurity professionals found that 86 percent agreed the government should mandate minimum standards for critical infrastructure companies.

"We have minimum standards for fire safety because there is collateral damage to adjacent structures from fires and limited public resources for fighting fires. We are now seeing the same risks coming to cybersecurity."[36]

—Chris Wysopal, chief technology officer at a cybersecurity firm

Mandating or creating incentives for reporting cyberincidents could also increase cybersecurity. Information on threats or attacks

Protect Yourself

To decrease your chances of falling victim to a cyberscam or cyber-attack, take care of basic cyberhygiene. Use complex and unique passwords and enable automatic software updates. Protect all your devices, not just computers and phones but also gaming consoles, printers, and anything else connected to a home network. Use antivirus software, firewalls, and when available, multifactor authentication. Do not click links or attachments from someone unknown. Keep data backups separate from your computer.

When it comes to cybersecurity, people and not devices are often the weakest link. The details may vary, but scams often use similar strategies. Cyberscammers will try to seem authentic. If you receive a message that appears to come from an organization you know, visit your online account instead of clicking a link in the message. Check unknown businesses or people online by searching their name with the words *scam* or *fraud*. Scammers will also entice or pressure you to act quickly. They may promise a prize or fabricate an emergency. Consult others before acting. Scammers often request money in gift cards. Do not buy one for anyone you do not personally know. If you become a victim, calling authorities can help protect others.

can help authorities pursue criminals and protect other targets. Although all states require reporting of personal data breaches, states and the federal government do not generally require companies to report ransomware, espionage, or other cyberattacks. Companies may fear that reporting will harm their reputation, invite future attacks, result in lawsuits, or slow the recovery process. Some business leaders find the reporting process confusing and time consuming. Mandating reporting and increasing information sharing could help organizations protect themselves and help policy makers better allocate resources to fight cybercrime and cyberattacks.

In 2021 Biden and the DHS issued new reporting requirements for critical pipeline owners and operators and for companies that supply technology services to federal agencies. Cyberattacks in 2021 also turned up the heat in Congress, which now bubbles with proposed cybersecurity legislation. Among many recently introduced bills are those that mandate or create incentives for additional critical infrastructure companies to report cyberincidents. Industry leaders say, however, that the government must do more than just collect information. "For a long time organizations have been providing information to the government. . . . The problem is that we rarely get anything back. . . . It needs to be a two-way street,"[37] says Jamil Farshchi, chief information security officer at the credit reporting agency Equifax. Sharing more information across sectors and adopting minimum standards could help deter attacks and build resilience.

Nation-States Working Better Together

Because cybercriminals carry out activities from around the world, reducing cyberscams and ransomware attacks requires international coordination. Cybercriminals sometimes work in one country to attack victims in another country, using servers from a third country. Gathering evidence from different jurisdictions can be time consuming because of legal and technical challenges. Better cooperation among law enforcement and intelligence agencies could help the United States and its allies identify, arrest, and prosecute ransomware criminals and cyberscammers.

Beyond solving logistical issues, reducing cybercrime requires dismantling safe havens. In some countries, governments ignore cybercrime targeted at foreign countries. They may do so for a bribe, in return for hacking services, or because local economies can benefit from criminal proceeds. Other countries lack the resources to take down criminal operations. The Ransomware Task Force, a coalition of cyberexperts from the government, research institutions, and business, recommends a combination of sanctions, incentives, and resources to motivate countries that willingly or unwittingly provide safe havens.

Extinguishing ransomware attacks will likely require changes in global cryptocurrency markets. "Cryptocurrency is the oxygen that fuels the ransomware fire, and we absolutely have to tackle it,"[38] says cybersecurity expert Dmitri Alperovitch. Criminals typically demand ransoms in cryptocurrency because transactions are difficult to link to individuals. Motivating or supporting countries to adopt or enforce stricter rules, similar to those for traditional currency, could help. Better international cooperation can deter ransomware attacks by making the proceeds less certain and punishment more certain.

Living with Cyberattacks

Even with better cooperation, nation-states are unlikely to give up cyberweapons. Adopting rules about their use could limit the collateral damage from cyberattacks. In 2017 Brad Smith, president of Microsoft, called for extending the Geneva Conventions to

Microsoft president and vice chair Brad Smith addresses an audience at the Web Summit 2021. Smith has called for the Geneva Conventions, a set of treaties that establish the ground rules for war, to be extended to cyberspace.

Cybersecurity Workers Badly Needed

There are more than 460,000 unfilled cybersecurity positions in the United States, according to CyberSeek, a website developed by the National Institute for Science and Technology. The gaping shortage of workers makes defending networks harder. The median pay for information security workers, $103,590, far outstrips the median for all occupations, $41,950, according to the Bureau of Labor Statistics. But the worker shortage does not show signs of reversing. The bureau predicts a 33 percent growth in information security jobs over the next ten years.

Filling the gap will require training current technology workers and increasing the number of students who choose a cybersecurity career. The federal government and major technology firms have committed resources to help. The American Rescue Plan, passed in 2021, gives $200 million to hire cybersecurity workers in the public sector. In 2021 IBM committed to train 150,000 cybersecurity workers over three years and to partner with historically Black colleges and universities to increase the diversity of the workforce. Microsoft and Google have also made pledges to train more workers. Without workers to protect networks, respond to attacks, and develop new cybersecurity technologies, defenders will continue to struggle.

cyberspace. The Geneva Conventions are a widely adopted set of international treaties that establish ground rules for war. Among other things, they protect medical personnel and noncombatant civilians. They also prohibit targeting civilian hospitals and medical transports. Speaking to the United Nations, Smith said, "The world needs a new digital Geneva Convention. It needs new rules of the road. What we need . . . is an approach that governments will adopt that says they will not attack civilians in times of peace. They will not attack hospitals. They will not attack the electrical grid. They will not attack the political processes of other countries."[39] Cyberattacks that affect hospitals, critical infrastructure, or elections would violate a digital Geneva Convention, as Smith has envisioned it. Whether a formal agreement or unspoken norms, some think nation-states should work together to decide what targets are off limits.

The United States can improve cybersecurity, but it may also need backup plans, at least for critical functions. The United States has three electric power grids, the Eastern, Western, and Texas grids. A cyberattack that damaged any one grid could cause significant problems for millions of people. Lights, heat, computer and phone chargers, and medical equipment, among other things, could stop working. In 2019 an attacker breached an electric utility. Although the hacker did not disrupt power, the attack demonstrated the vulnerability of the American electric grid. Clarke and Knake recommend a backup system with mini distribution networks disconnected from the main grids. The backup would include alternative sources of fuel. If a main grid went down, the networks could provide continuous power to critical entities like hospitals and military bases.

A significant cyberattack could also threaten the functioning of the military and economy. Clarke and Knake recommend that the military have communication systems that do not rely on the internet, weapons that do not require use of the Global Positioning System, and the ability to conduct warfare without the latest technological advances. The Cyberspace Solarium Commission also recommends a contingency plan for the economy in case of serious cyberattack. The United States could, for example, develop distribution plans for important goods and services and consider stockpiling critical raw materials and goods.

Having an open internet and connected world brings benefits and risks. Hardening targets or designating some off-limits increases the costs of launching cyberassaults. Coordinating with allies to find and prosecute criminals reduces the payoffs to cyberscams and ransomware attacks. Higher costs and lower payoffs will deter some assaults. However, sophisticated and motivated attackers, including nation-states, will still attempt them. Building resilience to quickly recover will improve the security of people, organizations, and countries. There is no end in sight to cyberscams and cyberattacks, but the defense can grow stronger.

Source Notes

Introduction: Cyberscams and Cyberattacks Surge

1. Quoted in Leila Fadel, "A Ransomware Attack Hit Up to 1,500 Businesses. A Cybersecurity Expert on What's Next," NPR, July 6, 2021. www.npr.org.
2. Cyberspace Solarium Commission, *Executive Summary*, 2020. www.solarium.gov.
3. Quoted in White House, "Remarks by President Biden at the Office of the Director of National Intelligence," July 27, 2021. www.whitehouse.gov.
4. Richard A. Clarke and Robert K. Knake, *The Fifth Domain: Defending Our Country, Our Companies, and Ourselves in the Age of Cyber Threats*. New York: Penguin, 2019, p. 297.

Chapter One: Cyberscams

5. Mark Button and Cassandra Cross, *Cyber Frauds, Scams and Their Victims*. New York: Routledge, 2017, p. 62.
6. Quoted in Marissa Parra, "'Something Was Not Right': Chicago Area Teen Warns of Job Scam Seeking Personal Information," CBS Chicago, July 1, 2021. https://chicago.cbslocal.com.
7. Quoted in Hugh Lessig, "'It Broke My Heart:' The Cruelty of Military Romance Scams," *Newport News (VA) Daily Press*, August 11, 2018. www.dailypress.com.
8. Quoted in Paula Span, "When Romance Is a Scam," *New York Times*, March 27, 2020. www.nytimes.com.
9. Quoted in Jon Emont, "This Year's Big Online Scam – Puppies," *Wall Street Journal*, September 2, 2020. www.wsj.com.
10. Quoted in NBC Bay Area, *Hackers Steal Millions from Bay Area Residents by Targeting Cellphones in "SIM Swap" Scams*, YouTube, May 29, 2019. www.youtube.com/watch?v=jc62Z8ABMeI.
11. Quoted in NBC Bay Area, *Hackers Steal Millions from Bay Area Residents by Targeting Cellphones in "SIM Swap" Scams*.

Chapter Two: Ransomware Attacks

12. Quoted in White House, *President Biden Delivers Remarks on the Colonial Pipeline Incident*, YouTube, May 13, 2021. www.youtube.com/watch?v=nGheL-pP_aI.
13. Quoted in Clare Duffy, "Wanted: Millions of Cybersecurity Pros. Salary: Whatever You Want," CNN, May 28, 2021. www.cnn.com.
14. Quoted in Benjamin Wittes, "Matt Tait Ransom 'Wears' All the Things," July 6, 2021, in *Lawfare Podcast*, produced by Jen Patja Howell, podcast. www.lawfareblog.com.
15. Quoted in C-Span, "Senate Homeland Security Hearing on Colonial Pipeline Cyber Attack," June 8, 2021. www.c-span.org.
16. Quoted in Terry Gross, "Inside the Ransomware Industry," *Fresh Air*, NPR, June 10, 2021. www.npr.org.
17. Quoted in Alan Blinder and Nicole Perlroth, "A Cyberattack Hobbles Atlanta, and Security Experts Shudder," *New York Times*, March 27, 2018. www.nytimes.com.
18. Kartikay Mehrotra, "The Anatomy of a Ransomware Attack," Bloomberg, June 15, 2021. www.bloomberg.com.

Chapter Three: Nation-State Attacks

19. Quoted in Dina Temple-Raston and Jacob Goldstein, "One Hack to Fool Them All," *Planet Money*, NPR, May 28, 2021. www.npr.org.
20. Clarke and Knake, *The Fifth Domain*, p. 21.
21. Clarke and Knake, *The Fifth Domain*, p. 188.
22. Quoted in Julianne Pepitone, "China Is 'Leading Suspect' in OPM Hacks, Says Intelligence Chief James Clapper," NBC News, June 25, 2015. www.nbcnews.com.
23. Quoted in Andy Greenberg, *Sandworm: A New Era of Cyberwar and the Hunt for the Kremlin's Most Dangerous Hackers*. New York: Doubleday, 2019, p. 188.
24. Ellen Nakashima and Shane Harris, "How the Russians Hacked the DNC and Passed Its Emails to WikiLeaks," *Washington Post*, July 13, 2018. www.washingtonpost.com.
25. Quoted in Dan Goodin, "NSA-Leaking Shadow Brokers Just Dumped Its Most Damaging Release Yet," Ars Technica, April 14, 2017. https://arstechnica.com.

Chapter Four: Defending Against Scams and Attacks

26. Quoted in Clarke and Knake, *The Fifth Domain*, p. 50.

27. Quoted in US Senate Committee on Homeland Security & Governmental Affairs, "Hearing Before the United States Senate Committee on Homeland Security & Governmental Affairs," June 8, 2021. www.hsgac.senate.gov.

28. Quoted in Clarke and Knake, *The Fifth Domain*, p. 42.

29. Richard J. Harknett, "United States Cyber Command's New Vision: What It Entails and Why It Matters," *Lawfare* (blog), March 23, 2018. www.lawfareblog.com.

30. Quoted in Andy Greenberg, "A Trickbot Assault Shows US Military Hackers' Growing Reach," *Wired*, October 14, 2020. www.wired.com.

31. Quoted in Steve Ranger, "Meet the Hackers Who Earn Millions for Saving the Web, One Bug at a Time," ZDNet, November 16, 2020. www.zdnet.com.

32. Quoted in Rachel Monroe, "How to Negotiate with Ransomware Hackers," *New Yorker*, June 7, 2021. www.newyorker.com.

33. Quoted in Ellen Nakashima, "Cyber Command Has Sought to Disrupt the World's Largest Botnet, Hoping to Reduce Its Potential Impact on the Election," *Washington Post*, October 9, 2020. www.washingtonpost.com.

Chapter Five: What More Can Be Done?

34. Quoted in NBC News, *Joe Biden's Full Press Conference After Putin Summit*, YouTube, June 16, 2021. www.youtube.com/watch?v=lOw_qT1ls6k.

35. Clarke and Knake, *The Fifth Domain*, p. 42.

36. Quoted in Joseph Marks, "The Cybersecurity 202: Our Expert Network Says It's Time for More Cybersecurity Regulations," *Washington Post*, June 11, 2021. www.washingtonpost.com.

37. Quoted in Susan Caminiti, "What Cybersecurity Leaders Say They Need from the Federal Government," CNBC, August 25, 2021. www.cnbc.com.

38. Quoted in Eric Geller, "Global 'Whack-a-Mole': Why It's so Hard for the U.S. to Go After Hackers' Digital Wallets," Politico, August 14, 2021. www.politico.com.

39. Quoted in *Microsoft Corporate Blogs*, "Brad Smith Takes His Call for a Digital Geneva Convention to the United Nations," Microsoft, November 9, 2017. https://blogs.microsoft.com.

Cyber Operations Tracker, Council on Foreign Relations
https://microsites-live-backend.cfr.org/cyber-operations
The Council on Foreign Relations is an independent research institute focused on international policy. The Cyber Operations Tracker provides details on nation-state cyberattacks since 2005. It includes a map and a tool to search attacks by type of operation, victim, and state sponsor.

CyberSeek
www.cyberseek.org
The National Institute of Standards and Technology sponsored the creation of this website to help employers, job seekers, and students better understand the cybersecurity job market. The website includes an interactive map, a career pathway tool, statistics, and job descriptions.

Darknet Diaries
https://darknetdiaries.com
Jack Rhysider developed the *Darknet Diaries* podcast to educate and entertain audiences about hacking and cybersecurity. Using journalistic standards and methods, Rhysider tells the stories of nation-state attacks, penetration testers, criminal hackers, and more.

Internet Crime Complaint Center (IC3), Federal Bureau of Investigation
www.ic3.gov
The FBI's IC3 collects and reports on complaints of cybercrimes from personal scams to ransomware. The website provides current news, alerts, annual reports with statistics, and tips for protecting individuals and businesses from cybercrime.

Lawfare Institute
www.lawfareblog.com
The Lawfare Institute hosts multiple podcasts and a blog focusing on issues of national security, including cybersecurity. The blog posts and podcasts feature leaders, experts, and policy makers discussing current cybersecurity news.

For Further Research

Books

Frank W. Abagnale, *Scam Me If You Can: Simple Strategies to Outsmart Today's Rip-Off Artists*. New York: Portfolio, 2019.

Richard A. Clarke and Robert K. Knake, *The Fifth Domain: Defending Our Country, Our Companies, and Ourselves in the Age of Cyber Threats*. New York: Penguin, 2019.

Andy Greenberg, *Sandworm: A New Era of Cyberwar and the Hunt for the Kremlin's Most Dangerous Hackers*. New York: Doubleday, 2019.

Nicole Perlroth, *This Is How They Tell Me the World Ends the Cyberweapons Arms Race*. New York: Bloomsbury, 2021.

Jeremy N. Smith, *Breaking and Entering: The Extraordinary Story of a Hacker Called "Alien."* Boston: Houghton Mifflin Harcourt, 2019.

Internet Resources

Better Business Bureau, *Online Scams Rise During COVID-19 Pandemic: 2020 BBB Scam Tracker Risk Report*, 2021. www.bbb.org.

Dorothy E. Denning, "Is Quantum Computing a Cybersecurity Threat?," *American Scientist*, vol. 107, no. 2, 2019. www.americanscientist.org.

Garrett M. Graff, "The Man Who Speaks Softly—and Commands a Big Cyber Army," *Wired*, October 13, 2020. www.wired.com.

Rachel Monroe, "How to Negotiate with Ransomware Hackers," *New Yorker*, May 31, 2021. www.newyorker.com.

Ransomware Task Force, *Combating Ransomware: A Comprehensive Framework for Action*, 2021. https://securityandtechnology.org.

Index